Post-Democracy

Also by Hannah Moscovitch

Post-Democracy
Hannah Moscovitch

Playwrights Canada Press
Toronto

Playwrights Canada Press
202-269 Richmond St. W., Toronto, ON M5V 1X1
416.703.0013 | info@playwrightscanada.com | www.playwrightscanada.com

LIBRARY AND ARCHIVES CANADA CATALOGUING IN PUBLICATION
Title: Post-democracy / Hannah Moscovitch.
Names: Moscovitch, Hannah, author.
Description: First edition.
Identifiers: Canadiana (print) 20220430233 | Canadiana (ebook) 20220430241
  | ISBN 9780369103666 (softcover) | ISBN 9780369103680 (PDF)
  | ISBN 9780369103673 (EPUB)
Subjects: LCGFT: Drama.
Classification: LCC PS8626.O837 P67 2022 | DDC C812/.6—dc23

Playwrights Canada Press operates on land which is the ancestral home of the
Anishinaabe Nations (Ojibwe / Chippewa, Odawa, Potawatomi, Algonquin,
Saulteaux, Nipissing, and Mississauga), the Wendat, and the members of the
Haudenosaunee Confederacy (Mohawk, Oneida, Onondaga, Cayuga, Seneca, and
Tuscarora), as well as Metis and Inuit peoples. It always was and always will be
Indigenous land.

We acknowledge the support of the Canada Council for the Arts, the Ontario Arts
Council (OAC), Ontario Creates, and the Government of Canada for our publishing
activities.

To my dad, Allan Moscovitch, again. And to my stepmom, Linda Goldberg.

Post-Democracy was first produced by Prairie Theatre Exchange as a digital-only production from April 8 to 25, 2021, with the following cast and creative team:

Shannon: Alicia Johnston
Lee: Kristian Jordan
Bill: Arne MacPherson
Justine: Stephanie Sy

Thomas Morgan Jones: Director
Brian Perchaluk: Set, Props, and Costume Design
Scott Henderson: Lighting Design
jaymez: Sound Design
Cherissa Richards: Artistic Associate
Julie Lumsden: PTE Directing Mentorship
Karyn Kumhyr: Stage Manager
Ali Fulmyk: Assistant Stage Manager
Sam Vint: Film Director
Sam Karney: Director of Photography
Andrew Weins: Camera/Editor
Rudy Gauer: Camera
John Hildebrand: Film Audio

The play was later produced by Tarragon Theatre, Toronto, in their Mainspace from November 8 to December 4, 2022, with the following cast and creative team:

Shannon: Rachel Cairns
Justine: Chantelle Han
Lee: Jesse LaVercombe
Bill: Diego Matamoros

Director: Mumbi Tindyebwa Otu
Set and Costume Designer: Teresa Przybylski
Lighting Designer: Louise Guinand
Sound Designer: John Gzowski
Stage Manager: Sandy Plunkett
Apprentice Stage Manager: Emma Jo Conlin

Punctuation.

Dash (—): a dash at the end of a line of dialogue indicates a cut-off.
Dash 2 (—): a dash in the middle a line of dialogue indicates a quick change in thought or a stutter.
Ellipsis (. . .): an ellipsis at the end of a line indicates a trail-off.
Ellipsis 2 (. . .): an ellipsis in the middle of a line indicates a hesitation or a mental search for a thought or a word.
Ellipsis 3 (. . . dialogue . . .) ellipses on either side of a line of dialogue indicates a person who is speaking over the other character or trying to interrupt the other character.
Slash (/): indicates the point at which the character that speaks next interrupts the character that is currently speaking.

Beat: approximately a one-count.
Pause: approximately a three-count.
Silence: approximately a six-count.

Notes.

The role of Justine was developed in consultation with Stephanie Sy.

The author's intention is that the play is a kind of hypernaturalism. Not kitchen-sink naturalism, but over-the-top naturalism in which we see the gross extremes of human behaviour: vomiting, alcohol-fuelled sexuality and self-pity, violent language, etc. The realism of this play should look and feel too up-close and too voyeuristic and too disgusting.

"Is he a payer or a receiver? So he wants free info? Tell you what: I want a blow job from Eva Mendes, and I'll tell you right now I'd be receiving."
—overheard on Bay Street

"Politics and government are increasingly slipping back into the control of privileged elites in the manner characteristic of pre-democratic times."
—Colin Crouch

Characters.

Bill, CEO and Chairman (sixties)
Lee, COO and Vice-President (early thirties, Bill's cousin many times removed)
Justine, CFO (early thirties, Bill's daughter)
Shannon, Director of Public Relations (mid-thirties to mid-forties, Justine's friend)

Scene One.

The lights snap up on the lounge. The lounge is neutral, under-stated, and elegant. It suggests maximum wealth. There are leather armchairs, a chaise longue, large feathery palm trees in heavy iron pots, and works of modern art.

BILL is on his iPhone. LEE holds a coffee. He tosses a couple of pills into his mouth, takes a swallow of coffee, grimaces.

Silence.

LEE waits while BILL scrolls.

LEE takes his iPhone out, checks it, then puts it away. He slowly gets impatient. Finally:

LEE: You got in yesterday, saw the . . . city . . . ?

BILL: I saw the highway between the airport and this hotel. It looked like . . . *(shrugs)* . . . a city.

LEE: Yeah, it's polluted, and poor, but it's fine.

Pause.

So, we meeting . . . ?

BILL: Yeah.

Beat.

But BILL's *still looking at his phone.*

Beat.

LEE: *(re:* BILL's *phone)* What—what's . . . ? Gary? The brand manager?

BILL: Yeah.

LEE: It was just a couple of comments? Wasn't it?

Beat.

What? Were they bad?

BILL: Well, they made the news.

LEE: Oh yeah? So: what? He said something stupid.

BILL: Yeah, he did.

LEE: Is that what you want to talk to me about?

BILL: *(low)* No.

BILL glances at the wall for a moment. Narrows his eyes at it. LEE *follows his gaze. Then* BILL *looks back down at his iPhone.*

LEE: What?

BILL looks up and points at the wall, then goes back to this device.

What . . . ?

BILL: They rent this art. I had this piece last year, in my foyer.

LEE: *(with some surprise)* You *rented* it.

BILL: Yeah, we rent at the office too. Did you think we own what's on the walls at the office? We don't: we rent it.

LEE: *(not interested)* Yeah?

BILL: You don't look at the art, at the office?

LEE shrugs.

What do we have in the lobby?

LEE: Art?

BILL: A Matisse.

LEE: Is that a thing?

BILL gives him an amused look.

What?

Silence: BILL goes back to his iPhone. LEE considers the piece of art. He tries to appreciate it. Finally, BILL pockets his phone and turns and looks at LEE, assessing him. Off BILL's look:

What!

BILL: How'd you sleep last night?

LEE: Fine.

Beat.

Fine: I worked until the last minute on this deal, flew in, got to find out how bad my Spanish is, made it to the hotel, I slept *three fucking hours in my fucking clothes* so I could come and meet you for a six a.m. meeting.

BILL: Well last night, I couldn't sleep.

LEE: Oh yeah.

> *Beat.*

> *Off BILL's gaze:*

Okay?

> *Beat.*

(mystified) You should try audiobooks.

> *Beat.*

> *Off BILL's glance:*

Books, fiction, you download them. *The Da Vinci Code*? Two minutes and you pass right out.

BILL: Well last night, I couldn't sleep . . .

LEE: . . . I'm telling you: audiobooks . . .

BILL: . . . I was up late, working: I heard knocking at the . . . door.

> *Beat.*

LEE: Oh yeah?

BILL: I opened it, and there was a girl standing there.

LEE: Yeah?

BILL: She said "hello," her name is . . . *(gestures)* . . . it was a, you know, local name—and she said she was from Systemas, and did I want her to come in?

LEE: *(suggestive)* Oh yeah?

Beat.

(suggestive) So you uh . . . ?

BILL: She was a teenager.

Beat.

LEE: *(suggestive)* Oh *yeah?*

Beat. BILL regards LEE.

What—what?

BILL: Lee.

LEE: What!

Beat.

What?

Beat.

No! No, apparently the coo doesn't get a teenager. Or I slept through it: I took a late flight, got to the hotel, then I was out—

BILL: We're getting enough attention as it is . . .

BILL gestures to his iPhone.

LEE: . . . Yeah . . .

BILL: . . . So let's not . . .

LEE: . . . Yeah: I find my own fun . . .

BILL: . . . I'm saying—no, I'm saying: don't have any fun. All right? Let's, please, stay away from the minors.

LEE: She wasn't a minor.

BILL: Yeah, she was.

LEE: There's no such thing as a minor here. It's not illegal, for instance, to . . .

Beat.

What?

BILL: *(a joke)* As far as I know, this *is* a country: they have a criminal code, they have an age of consent—

LEE: *(sarcasm)* Sure they do.

BILL: Lee.

LEE: And you don't know she was a teenager.

BILL: Pretty sure.

LEE: How?

BILL: Looked at her. With the eyes in my face.

LEE: But come on, she wasn't *twelve*, fuck! That's if it even *was* the same . . .

BILL realizes what LEE is saying: that he's confessing.

(confessing) . . . girl.

Beat.

I just—I wasn't thinking . . .

Beat.

I—yeah—I got in late—I wasn't thinking.

Beat.

Sorry.

Pause.

BILL shakes his head.

BILL: Yeah . . . No, you have to curb this.

LEE: I have to curb *what*?

Beat.

I'm not going to do anything that would . . . ! I've even stopped hitting on Shannon. It's my new management style: I've decided not to fuck the employees. I'm trying to think outside the box. Well not outside the *box*.

LEE grins.

(off BILL's look) To be clear: I'd like to hit on Shannon. But I'm not, because: company policy, and also, you said to me, "Don't fuck Shannon." Or, "Don't intercourse Shannon," or whatever you said.

    Beat.

I'm not going to do anything that would in any way . . . hurt the company.

    Pause.

Can I *go?*

    Beat: a standoff.

BILL: I want this deal to go through—

    LEE turns to go.

No, Lee.

    LEE turns back.

The board likes it, the shareholders'll like it, and then I'm going to . . . step down for a few months . . .

LEE: . . . What! When? . . .

BILL: . . . So please.

    Beat.

LEE: Why? Why! Are you . . . ? Why! Are you . . . all right?

    Beat.

Bill?

Beat.

Bill?

BILL: Probably.

LEE: What does that mean?

BILL shrugs.

Pause.

Like . . . what . . . like . . . something . . . bad, like . . . ? Cancer?

Pause.

Cancer?

Beat.

BILL: It's cancer.

Beat.

LEE: Does Justine know?

Beat.

No?

BILL: Not yet.

LEE: Holy shit.

Beat.

I'm sorry.

BILL nods.

Then BILL gets out his iPhone and starts scrolling.

Are you saying I'll . . . I'll be interim . . . CEO?

Beat.

BILL looks up at him.

BILL: That's what I'm hoping. The board likes this deal, and they like you. So I'm here, to see Systemas. If it works out . . . *(gestures)* . . . Should help convince the board that you're . . . the right fit.

Beat.

Yeah?

LEE: Yeah. Yeah!

Beat.

And that's it, that's the whole talk?

BILL: Yeah.

LEE: Okay. Wow.

BILL gives him a look, then glances back down at his phone. Meanwhile, LEE's stunned.

The circumstances are . . . so bad. But uh, uh, uh, well, thanks?

BILL *doesn't respond.*

End scene.

Scene Two.

BILL, LEE, and JUSTINE all sit or stand in the lounge. JUSTINE is expensively dressed: high heels, power suit, and lipstick. All three of them hold drinks: martinis, Scotches. All three scroll on their phones. Finally, LEE looks up at BILL and JUSTINE expectantly.

LEE: So: Systemas?

Pause.

So, guys, Systemas?

Pause.

Guys, Systemas: Is the company that you were here to tour—we toured it—what did you think?

Beat.

It was soooo good, what a good company: we should buy it—

JUSTINE: *(to LEE)* Sorry, I'm reading about *our* company, in the news.

(to BILL) Are you looking at this? Dad?

BILL: Yeah.

JUSTINE: This is crazy.

BILL: Yeah.

JUSTINE: *(reading)* . . . "A senior executive frequently sent his executive assistant texts telling her he needed her to be the 'T and A at table' when he was meeting buyers. T and A stood for tits and ass. One time he followed her into the women's washroom and looked over the top of her stall while she was urinating as a"—quote unquote—"joke. Also as a"—quote unquote—"joke, he sometimes cornered her on business trips and made advances, telling her to make up for her lack of competence on the job by—"

Okay, this is that brand manager?

BILL: Yeah.

JUSTINE: Gary . . . ?

BILL: Yeah.

JUSTINE: And the assistant, who's she?

    BILL shrugs.

Did she go to HR?

BILL: *(nods)* We've fired a couple of HR people: the ones who said her complaint didn't strike them as . . .

    BILL gestures.

Of consequence.

JUSTINE: *Shit.*

BILL: Yeah.

JUSTINE: But what . . . ? Shouldn't we be on flights home?

LEE looks up, worried.

BILL: *(to JUSTINE, shrugging)* We're not answering media requests, that's Shannon's department. She's set up a PR camp back home, all interviews go through her. That's the only big one so far. And Connor's there—

LEE: Connor's there?

BILL: To handle any legal.

LEE: Uh? Don't we need Connor here? To handle the contracts?

JUSTINE: I'm handling them. I've got the contracts.

(to BILL) Shannon said there was a story out—I didn't realize how bad.

LEE: Don't we ?

JUSTINE: I have them, I have them!

(to BILL) Dad, what's . . . ? Why aren't we on flights home?

LEE makes a jerky, frustrated motion with his body and walks away.

BILL and JUSTINE look at LEE.

What? This seems like it might be about to . . . turn into a media frenzy?

LEE: *(to JUSTINE, rhetorical)* Is it affecting stock prices?

JUSTINE looks over at BILL.

Beat.

BILL: A small dip, but that could be . . .

BILL gestures, vague . . .

Beat.

LEE stares at JUSTINE.

JUSTINE: Okay! Okay.

LEE: *(to JUSTINE)* What?

JUSTINE: There are always guys like you who say "twenty-four-hour news cycle" and "it won't affect stock prices" . . .

LEE: . . . I didn't say that . . .

JUSTINE: . . . And sometime that's true . . .

LEE: . . . Except I didn't say it . . .

JUSTINE: . . . And sometimes they come into your office and take away the furniture.

LEE: So: Systemas. Let's buy Systemas, okay? Come on, that tour was a victory lap, it was pitch perfect. Let's get these contracts signed, then we can fly back home and turn our business into a woke sandbox. We can be all, "Rah rah, decolonize the workplace, queer our content, it's never funny when you punch down, no one misgendered in our office, grind our own oat milk!" And I'm all for giving days off for your period cramps, Justine, since you're a "person who bleeds"—

BILL: Lee.

LEE: *(to BILL)* Well she's . . . !

JUSTINE: *(to LEE)* I'm what?

> *Beat.*

I'm what?

> *Beat.*

> *LEE shrugs.*

> *Beat.*

Take a look at Silicon Valley . . .

LEE: . . . Cool cool, I'll "take a look at it" . . .

JUSTINE: . . . And what's happened to the stocks of companies with reputations of sexual harassment . . .

LEE: . . . They bounce back.

JUSTINE: Not when it's the CEO . . .

LEE: . . . Well, it's not.

JUSTINE: . . . Or a pivotal exec: okay, fine fine, that's your . . . fine.

> *Beat.*

I mean . . . !

> *Beat.*

(to BILL) Some executive assistant's trying to do her job, and that's the shit that's . . . ?

BILL: Yeah.

JUSTINE: That's what we want. We want to be one of those companies with women crying in the bathroom because some fucking . . . brand manager . . . ?

Beat.

BILL's phone buzzes.

He looks down at it.

BILL: I'm sorry, it's Connor. I have to take this.

BILL walks to the back of the lounge, takes the call.

BILL stays in the background, speaking simultaneously with JUSTINE and LEE in the foreground.

(*into phone, low*) Yeah.

Beat.

Yeah.

Pause.

That's . . . yeah what I'm trying to set up.

Beat.

Yeah.

Beat.

Thanks. And this is still . . . yeah.

Simultaneous to the above, in the foreground, JUSTINE and LEE speak.

JUSTINE scrolls, shaking her head.

Pause.

LEE: *(to JUSTINE)* Hey, Justine, hey, I know: hey, Justine, you know what would help? Why don't you make a media statement about your Africa projects. "I just—it is such a vital continent! It's just so . . . alive, you know? You just have to go there to get a sense of what it's like *on the ground*!"

Beat.

JUSTINE: You're making fun of my charity work.

LEE: No, I think it's great you're getting involved. Flying your private jet over Africa.

In the background, BILL hangs up his call and walks back toward JUSTINE and LEE.

JUSTINE: *(to LEE)* Yeah? What's *your* charity work?

LEE: Well, I've been trying not to park my Maserati in the disabled parking spot at work, but it's just—it's so close to the door.

JUSTINE: Hunh. I thought "helping some young women work their way through college" would be more your thing—

LEE: Funny! Funny and charitable.

JUSTINE: How come you're making fun of me.

LEE: Uhhhhh? Because it's easy to? 'Cause you're a spoiled little bitch, and you only kind of know that about yourself?

JUSTINE: Dad.

BILL: Lee.

LEE points between JUSTINE and BILL.

LEE: That's my point!

BILL: Lee.

JUSTINE: How am I spoiled!? 'Cause I do charity work!?

LEE: Justine. You adopted a *village*. In Africa.

JUSTINE: So I'm spoiled because I do *a lot* of charity work?

BILL: Lee.

LEE: What? Come on. What? I'm not allowed to squabble with Justine?

JUSTINE: What's that mean?

LEE: What's what mean?

JUSTINE: Has Dad already told you off for something?

Beat.

LEE: I like Systemas. I liked the tour this morning: this is my seventh tour and I'm glad you joined me. Systemas has dealt with comparable companies to ours, including automotive parts companies. We'll have a subsidiary that isn't across an ocean. We have the contracts—I had Connor working on them up until the last minute—everything's finalized pending this tour. You've had a chance now to see their factories and facilities: I'm confident that we can move our operations here, and that this will be a cost-saving move, and a plus for our board and shareholders.

Beat.

Bill?

BILL: *(to JUSTINE)* Justine?

JUSTINE shrugs. Pause.

LEE: We're being priced out of China—

JUSTINE: How will it look when we drop our manufacturers?

LEE: It'll look like fuck all, because it's China, and no one gives a fuck about China. We could—when was the last time you were in Shenzhen?—we could cement over the whole fucking city on the way out and no one would give a fuck. I have a lot of hours in on this deal, including on "perception of the move."

JUSTINE: Dad?

BILL: Mm?

Beat.

BILL is pale and sick.

JUSTINE: You okay?

BILL: Yah. Yep.

LEE: You uh . . . Bill?

JUSTINE: You okay, Dad?

LEE: You all right?

BILL: Yeah, yep: just uh . . . yeah, tired.

> *Beat.*

> *BILL, pale, gestures for them to carry on.*

Justine.

JUSTINE: *(to BILL)* I . . . yeah, I . . . am at the board meetings—the board's enthusiastic—and yeah, I looked over the budgets and the cost structure is better. Obviously now we'll own our own manufacturing. But China's stable, and the political climate in South America being this volatile . . .

LEE: . . . Oh come on, it's fine . . .

JUSTINE: *(to BILL)* . . . I can't get a number out of "geopolitical uncertainty," and "the rise of populism in South America." And Dad? Now there's a scandal breaking—we don't know how big, and then we're / overextended?

LEE: Justine, Justine, Justine?

> *Beat.*

JUSTINE: Yeah?

LEE: Why don't you like the deal?

> *Beat.*

Why don't you?

> *Beat.*

Come on.

BILL: Justine?

Beat.

JUSTINE: *(low)* Are you friends with that brand manager, Lee?

Beat.

LEE: No!

Beat.

No. Not—no!

JUSTINE: A few parties?

LEE: No!

Beat.

JUSTINE: He's your type of guy . . .

LEE: . . . What! . . .

JUSTINE: He is.

LEE: . . . This is so stupid . . .

JUSTINE: I know you've been at parties with him: you went to Vegas with him . . .

LEE: . . . Sure, yes, I have.

Beat.

I have.

JUSTINE: Unhunh? What happened in Vegas?

LEE: We gambled.

JUSTINE: And then . . .

LEE: We . . . called a couple of our cousins to come over and play board games with us and then we said our prayers and went to bed.

JUSTINE: Yeah. That's what I thought.

LEE gazes back at her, stymied.

Beat.

JUSTINE turns to BILL and gestures, "See, I told you so."

Back in the '80s you could party with whores and video cameras—

LEE: *(to JUSTINE)* Do you think, for some reason, I was there in the '80s?

JUSTINE: *(to LEE)* I think you're part of that culture, yeah.

LEE: I'm part of '80s culture.

JUSTINE: *(to BILL)* And I think Lee's going to drag you into a corner, Dad, and he's going to say something like, "Hey, we're cousins five times removed" . . .

LEE: . . . That's not . . . !

JUSTINE: . . . "Let's go build a car together with our bare hands: the leather interiors will make us feel like we lassoed the bull ourselves, and you know what's funny: we couldn't convince the intern to have sex with us, so we had sex with her anyway." I think Lee's default is to laugh this off, laugh off the brand manager—

LEE: It was just a couple of comments!

Beat.

It's a joke, I'm joking.

JUSTINE: No you weren't.

LEE rolls his eyes, walks away.

Beat.

(to LEE) That's my problem with the deal.

LEE: *What is?*

JUSTINE: Well, it's a big deal—

LEE: Yeah, I'll have more sway, that's what you don't like.

Beat.

You'll have to raise a glass to me at board meetings.

Beat.

Come on.

Beat.

Come on.

Beat.

You don't want me to have more sway.

JUSTINE: You're the COO, you have tons of "sway"—

LEE: You don't want me to have *more.*

JUSTINE: *(to BILL)* I'm the Chief Financial Officer . . .

LEE: . . . Oh, cool, cool, we're just saying our titles now? . . .

JUSTINE: *(to BILL)* . . . I'm insulated, but even I'm aware that there's a shitty outdated culture at our company and Lee's going to come in, and none of that's going to change, because that's his culture, and our company'll / be this bloated old piece of shit . . . !

LEE: *(half to himself)* I don't use the family connection.

    BILL and JUSTINE look at him.

I don't.

    Beat.

(to JUSTINE) You use it, though.

JUSTINE: Unhunh?

LEE: You do.

JUSTINE: So I only got my job because of who my dad is?

LEE: It is.

    Beat.

It is why.

Beat.

I'm not saying you're not qualified, but it is how you got your job.

JUSTINE: And how'd you get your job? Because while you're qualified, you're also my dad's fifth cousin.

LEE: *(to BILL)* I want to sign with Systemas. Please. Please let me contribute this manufacturing deal to our company's health and growth. I worked hard on it, I'm happy with it: Bill?

BILL: Justine?

LEE: Can we sign now?

Beat.

Come on, we're going to sign, aren't we?

JUSTINE: Dad.

LEE: *(to JUSTINE)* Dad? What does "Dad" mean, in this context?

BILL: Lee.

LEE: What!?

JUSTINE: *(to BILL)* Dad?

Before BILL can respond, SHANNON comes in.

SHANNON: I'm sorry to interrupt . . . ?

BILL: No, Shannon: come in.

LEE: Yeah, Shannon, come on in. Come be the "tits and ass at table."

SHANNON glances at LEE briefly.

JUSTINE: That's not funny.

LEE: Uhhunh. What is still funny, Justine? Is it puns?

BILL: Shannon?

SHANNON: Uh yes. I'm sorry this isn't good news. The brand manager, Gary Sinclair, harassed another one of his executive assistants, although—nothing . . . too bad—and so far it's only come out internally.

Beat.

BILL: Yeah?

SHANNON: Gary sent a couple of emails to some of the other execs, at our company, about how they . . . at a massage parlour . . . they . . . engaged in . . . in . . . uh . . . I'm sorry, I'm blanking on the appropriate term for . . . uh . . . manual . . . uh . . . ?

Beat.

LEE: Hand job?

SHANNON: Uh, no: it's—I think it's . . .

Beat.

LEE: What is it?

SHANNON: . . . "Manual stimulation"?

LEE: *(as in "interesting")* Mm!

SHANNON: *(to BILL)* So look: Gary copied his executive assistant on those emails. Gary knows she's copied on those emails, but she does have access to all his emails, to his children, for instance, about school field trips to the museum, so it's . . . plausible he didn't think of it, at least initially. But when the exec assistant spoke to Gary about it and said, "I'm getting your emails about massage parlours," Gary found it funny. I spoke with her, Connor spoke with her, and she's going to sign an NDA.

BILL: Thank you.

    SHANNON smiles.

LEE: Shannon, you think this means we should wait on this deal, see if it blows up, see how it affects stock prices?

SHANNON: No? Why?

JUSTINE: Because there's a brand manager who's sexually harassing women, and we don't know how big it's going to break—

SHANNON: Well I'm hoping . . . ? I'm hoping to contain it?

JUSTINE: And if you can't?

    Beat.

SHANNON: Well—

JUSTINE: Not because you're not good at your job.

    Beat.

SHANNON: Uh, well—

JUSTINE: If you were assessing it for me, as your friend.

SHANNON: Uh—

JUSTINE: Like, when I used to call you for help before you were hired here?

SHANNON: Okay but—

JUSTINE: And you were able to say which companies were probably fucked—

SHANNON: Well, I think the exec assistant who came forward should not have had to go through that. But the worst incidents were contained to her. We've reached out to three other exec assistants who worked for Gary to ask, delicately, what . . . ? What their experience was like on the job. We've heard back from all three—one reported the massage parlour emails, and the other two were fine. Look, if the scandal was . . . higher up, wider . . . ?

LEE glances at BILL, and then turns and walks away.

JUSTINE: *(to SHANNON)* And what about our corporate culture?

SHANNON: *(nodding)* Well, those changes can happen gradually.

JUSTINE: *(suddenly furious)* AND HOW, SHANNON, ARE THEY GOING TO HAPPEN?

LEE: *(to JUSTINE)* Well don't yell at *her*?

BILL: *(to JUSTINE, to restrain her)* Honey, come on.

JUSTINE: No! I want a plan for how these gradual "corporate cultural changes" are actually going to happen because: *they're* not going to happen.

BILL: Honey—

JUSTINE: *(to SHANNON)* And I know you well enough to know you say shit like that and you don't really have any idea what it means.

SHANNON: *(to JUSTINE)* I . . . that's not my . . . job?

JUSTINE: Well whose job is it?

LEE: *(to BILL)* Mmmmmrrrrr! Can we sign?

Beat.

We're going to sign, aren't we? We're buying Systemas?

BILL: Let's . . .

Beat.

Let's pick this up in the morning.

Beat.

LEE: *(to BILL)* Okay. Yeah. I'm sorry to add to the . . .

JUSTINE smiles.

What are you smiling at?

BILL: *(as a warning)* Justine.

Silence as BILL and JUSTINE go out. Once they're gone SHANNON and LEE look at each other for a long moment, then:

LEE: How's your day going, Shannon?

SHANNON goes and lies face down on the couch.

Let's get loaded.

SHANNON turns her head and smiles.

End scene.

Scene Three.

There are empty glasses strewn all over the floor of the lounge. SHANNON and LEE make out on the chaise longue. It's very sexual: we hear the wet sound of them kissing. LEE is drunk. So is SHANNON, but not as drunk as LEE.

LEE: Mm yeah.

LEE and SHANNON make out. It should be simultaneously sexy and gross to the audience, or oscillating between sexy and gross.

Ten seconds of this.

Mm.

LEE starts to hike SHANNON's skirt up, somewhat clumsily (he's drunk), somewhat expertly (he's had a lot of practise). Just as LEE is about to pull SHANNON's skirt up too high for good taste and the audience starts to get uncomfortable:

SHANNON: Lee. Lee, Lee—

SHANNON pushes her skirt down and tries to disentangle herself, but LEE holds onto her.

LEE: *(feeling her trying to get away)* Mm no—Shannon Shannon—no, come here . . .

SHANNON: . . . Lee . . .

LEE: *(still holding her)* . . . Because you are *hot*. I want to fuck you. I want to fuck you *twice*.

SHANNON: Sh!

LEE: I want to eat / you out.

SHANNON: *(looking toward the door)* SSSSHHHHH!

LEE: Do you like that term or not: I wanna use the terms you / like—what?

SHANNON: Jesus, shhhhh!

LEE: No, but, come here / because—

SHANNON: Let's go back to your room.

LEE: No, no, 'cause I have a lot of sexual anticipation for this time with you—

SHANNON: Let's go to your room, though.

LEE: Shannon, sit down, 'cause I am your boss—help me to help you, Shannon.

SHANNON: *(laughing)* Oh my god!

    SHANNON gets up and pulls LEE to his feet. He sways.

LEE: Okay. Where can I puke? I need to sit down—sit down with me, Shannon—

SHANNON: No, come on, we're going—

LEE: No, you need to sit down and listen . . .

SHANNON: . . . No . . .

LEE: . . . Listen to this story that I'm going to tell / you.

SHANNON: Sh!

LEE: Sh!

SHANNON: *(laughing)* SH!!

LEE: SHHHHH! Shannon! Quiet, okay, fuck! Do want to hear my story or not? Because I am trying to give you a piece of myself, Shannon, okay, and that is true. So remember when we were in Shenzhen?

SHANNON: Yeah, Lee, I remember / Shenzhen . . .

LEE: So okay, I was in this strip club in Shenzhen—

SHANNON: *(frustration)* Lee!

LEE: No don't roll your eyes at *strip club* because . . .

SHANNON: *(almost to herself, low)* . . . I'm not rolling my eyes at strip club . . .

LEE: . . . You don't understand because it's nice to have a beer with tits in the background.

SHANNON: Okay, come on, get up, tell me your story back in your room—

LEE: No, no, I'm fucking—I'm talking: don't interrupt. I'm in this strip club and . . .

SHANNON: . . . Lee . . .

LEE: . . . Everyone is in this Shenzhen strip club, the whole fucking c-suite, and we're like "building rapport" with these Chinese execs and it's Shenzhen so there are people fucking the strippers in the corners . . .

SHANNON: . . . Who're you talking about . . . ?

LEE: And—no, don't do your job—and I was wandering around, and it was public sex and I . . .

SHANNON: . . . Jesus, Lee, you can't just tell me that: was it anyone from our company . . .

LEE: . . . Listen—I wasn't like, "Oh good, public sex, I should have some," I was like, "I wonder where Shannon is—I have to get out of here and go find Shannon," because I feel like—not like ahhhh get a crush on someone so it's palatable to go into the office, I mean like: can we do this, like not just the sex, like the other stuff like sex where we like make eye contact, can we do that sex?

SHANNON: Sure: first we have to get to your room—

LEE: Like I like watch you all the time at the office, like I feel this pull toward you that's like a movie, like you walk in and the air fills with . . . confetti, and I'm not allowed to because company policy, but, Shannon, I think we're a match, and like why don't you quit your job and I'll like buy us a scenic property to live in together 'cause I gotta curb this . . .

    LEE gestures toward himself.

. . . this whole . . .

SHANNON: Lee, you can't even stand.

    SHANNON tries to stand up and get off the chaise longue. LEE holds her, but she gets away.

LEE: Shannon. Shannon, no, stay, stay.

SHANNON: No, I'm not / staying . . .

LEE: No, if I just sit here with you, I will sober up—

SHANNON: No, you're way too drunk for / this . . .

LEE: Sit here—yes—sit yourself right here on the chaise longue, just sit your ass right down under this incomprehensible piece of art because I am very good at sex—

SHANNON: *(frustrated)* Lee! If you wanted to *fuck me*, you could have stopped at, like, say, four cocktails and the bottle of wine.

LEE: I am SOBERING UP!

SHANNON: LEE, HOLY SHIT! I had a—*do you know what I did today?* I talked an exec assistant into signing an NDA, long distance, on the phone, for *hours* . . . !

LEE: . . . I'm . . .

SHANNON: . . . AND THEN she sent me this email chain from Gary about an Asian spa, and they all talk about Justine in it—a girl at the massage parlour looked just like *Justine and they're all trying to book her and fuck the boss's daughter or whatever*—and do I disclose to someone that Justine's all over these emails? I can't tell Justine, right? That makes me a bad friend? And the whole time this exec assistant's crying. *She read some emails.* Like what the fuck, a lot worse things happen than some emails. It was hard to sit there listening to her cry, like don't you know *bad things happen!* I've had bad things happen to me—

LEE: Like what?

SHANNON: And I couldn't tell her how stupid she sounded.

LEE: What bad things?

SHANNON: And I could tell she liked the attention, and she liked having a thing she could complain about and be listened to about—

LEE: What bad things?

SHANNON: And now I'm sitting here with you in this lounge, and I want to fuck you. All I'm asking for is to go up to one of our hotel rooms so we aren't fucking in a lounge.

LEE: It's our lounge for our floor that only we are on.

SHANNON: Hotel staff could just walk in?

LEE: So what? So they'll watch: they don't matter . . . ?

SHANNON: Like with my ass in the air.

LEE: That's how you want it? That's how? It is?

SHANNON: Yeah, maybe.

LEE: But like do you like me more than just a fuck in a hotel?

SHANNON: *(a come on)* I don't know, Lee: there are some things I don't know about you yet, like how big's your dick?

LEE: Uh, I'm too drunk. Uh god—I'm—uh—I'm sorry, okay?

SHANNON: Yeah, I know.

LEE: I am so sorry.

SHANNON: That's okay, let's just . . . do this another / time—

LEE: I am just so sorry for . . . ! But I mean, come on! She will bounce back.

    Beat.

It was so easy to do it—I was so tired—I sat beside this guy with an obesity problem on the flight. He was just all over me with his fat, eating fucking cheese, and then I get here, it's the middle of the night, and I have not slept. I fucking can't even get my contacts out, they are glued on my eyeballs, and you know what? I did it and you know what: she was . . . *fine*—they bounce back at that age, they can take a little . . . !

SHANNON: What are you talking about?

LEE: And now I'm in the doghouse—well fuck him—I've been killing myself for that guy, pushing through this deal . . .

    Pause.

SHANNON: *(trying to work it out)* What did you . . . do?

LEE: I would un-fuck her if I could. I would *un-fuck her*.

SHANNON: What?

LEE: *(defensive)* WHAT? Okay? WHAT? WHAT . . .

SHANNON: What are you saying, are you saying . . . ?

LEE: . . . Uhhhh . . . can . . . water . . . ?

SHANNON: Okay. Okay.

    SHANNON stumbles around looking for some water for LEE.

LEE: *(urgent)* Water water!

SHANNON: I . . . am looking for it . . . I think there's some in here . . .

LEE: . . . Uh . . .

> *SHANNON hands LEE a paper cup. LEE drinks it. He looks, for a split second, like the water helped. But then he turns and barfs good and hard over the side of the chaise longue. SHANNON jumps out of the way.*

SHANNON: *(quiet, disgusted)* Uh god.

> *LEE lies there moaning, trying to recover, holding his stomach, spit dripping out of his mouth.*

LEE: Uh. Uh.

> *LEE spits a couple of times over the side of the chaise, onto the plush carpeting. SHANNON winces.*

> *Then LEE curls up, sick. SHANNON stands there, motionless, staring at LEE, trying to reckon with what she's just heard.*

Uh.

> *Beat.*

(barely audible, slurred) Uh sorry.

> *End scene.*

Scene Four.

*BILL, JUSTINE, LEE, and SHANNON are in the lounge. There is pain-
ful morning light. No sound other than air conditioning. LEE
and SHANNON are hungover and red-eyed, but dressed in business
clothes.*

JUSTINE: *(to BILL)* Um, okay, so, I'll talk.

Beat.

(to BILL) I was asleep—three in the morning, Shannon . . . pounded
on my door, and . . . kicked my door. She was . . . intoxicated, and
uh . . . not yelling but . . . *(gestures)* . . . I made her a coffee, I tried to
get her in the shower. She had vomit on her, on her dress, which she
said was Lee's vomit. She told me she'd been having a—a—a sexual
encounter with Lee, and at some point during it, he . . . ?

JUSTINE turns and looks at SHANNON.

So BILL and LEE turn and look at SHANNON as well.

All eyes on SHANNON.

SHANNON: *(half to LEE, half to BILL)* I told Justine that, last night,
Lee . . .

Beat.

LEE: *(to SHANNON)* What?

JUSTINE: *(to BILL)* She told me Lee said—

SHANNON: *(to BILL)* Lee was uh, uh . . .

JUSTINE: Blackout drunk—

SHANNON: So I don't know if what I remember / Lee saying is what he said or . . .

JUSTINE: *(to SHANNON)* Shannon, Shannon, SHANNON, SHANNON . . . !

(to BILL) There was a girl. There was a girl who Lee had relations with. This girl was not of legal age. And it sounds as though Lee . . . hurt this girl.

   Beat.

   JUSTINE looks at BILL.

Dad?

   LEE looks at SHANNON. BILL looks at LEE.

   LEE throws his hands up and walks away.

SHANNON: *(to LEE, low, almost mouthing it, rueful)* Sorry.

   But LEE is shaking his head, facing away from them.

   Beat.

JUSTINE: Dad?

BILL: Yeah.

JUSTINE: Dad?

Beat.

I'm a mother, and I . . .

Beat.

BILL: Yeah.

Beat.

JUSTINE: In one of my clinics, in Africa, there was a twelve-year-old girl and she had a perforated—her intestines were spilling into her *vagina.* Her body was just too small. And I was like: "Who could do this to her?"

JUSTINE works to control herself, then:

(turning back to BILL) This girl, she might be badly—she might be in some back room, with no water. A young girl: she might not even know what's happening to her. She might not go find a doctor . . . ?

Beat.

JUSTINE turns to LEE.

(to LEE) And also, *how could you, Lee?*

LEE: I didn't—I didn't do anything! And what you're describing is insane.

JUSTINE: Yeah?

Beat.

Dad?

Beat.

BILL: Yeah, I'm . . . yeah.

    Beat.

LEE: You okay?

BILL: *(to LEE)* Yeah, I'm . . . yeah. Lee?

LEE: Yeah?

BILL: Was she . . . ?

LEE: What?

BILL: Was she hurt?

    Beat.

LEE: What're you talking about?

    Beat.

What?

BILL: Just . . .

LEE: What?

    Beat.

Really?

BILL: Yeah.

    LEE shakes his head again.

Go ahead.

LEE: FINE! Fine.

    LEE turns to JUSTINE.

(calm but with menace) She was fine, Justine. She knew exactly what was happening to her. I paid her, she left—she walked out: she looked fine to me—

JUSTINE: She walked out? What do you mean "she walked out."

LEE: She stood up and she—

JUSTINE: She *stood up*?

    Beat.

What did you do to her?

LEE: *(to JUSTINE) I fucked her.*

BILL: *Lee.*

LEE: What?

BILL: Come on.

LEE: You want me to tell her: I'm telling her.

BILL: Let's keep it clean.

LEE: *(calmer)* She seemed fine to me. I paid her, she left, she walked out.

JUSTINE: She walked out!

LEE: Yeah? She was co-operative—

JUSTINE: *She was . . . ! She was co-operative?*

LEE: *(to JUSTINE)* Well you're asking me. I'm telling you.

JUSTINE: *(to BILL)* He told Shannon that there was an injury to the girl.

SHANNON: No.

JUSTINE: You said / there was a . . . !

SHANNON: *(to JUSTINE)* Yeah but I don't remember saying that *or anything*! My hands are all scraped up—I must have fallen on my hands—I don't remember *that*. I woke up in your sweatpants: I don't remember how I got into your sweatpants.

BILL: Justine, I think the girl's all right.

LEE: *(to himself, dismissing the event)* She was fine . . . !

    JUSTINE and BILL look at LEE. LEE sees them looking at him.

If I said anything to Shannon, I said they sent her to my room, she was standing outside my hotel room, and somehow I'm supposed to know that she's . . . ? They sent her to my room: someone out there thought she was the right one to send to me.

JUSTINE: Was she small?

LEE: No . . . !

JUSTINE: Was she . . . full grown?

LEE: *(too vehement)* Yes!

JUSTINE: How do you know?

LEE: She had tits?

BILL: Lee.

LEE: I mean . . . what? I mean, that's what she's asking?

JUSTINE: Was she an adult?

LEE: Why don't you ask them that? Why don't you ask the people who sent her to me those questions?

JUSTINE: BECAUSE YOU SHOULD KNOW BETTER.

LEE: Than who? Than them?

JUSTINE: YES.

LEE: I should know better than they do.

JUSTINE: YES.

LEE: Why?

JUSTINE: YOU SHOULD KNOW BETTER. YOU WERE NOT RAISED HERE, YOU WERE NOT RAISED IN THESE SLUMS, OKAY. YOU SHOULD KNOW BETTER THAN THESE PEOPLE—

LEE: THESE PEOPLE—

JUSTINE: THAN THESE—YES—THAN THESE PEOPLE WHO HAVE NOTHING. YOU HAVE *EVERYTHING*.

LEE: SHE'S A THIRD-WORLD WHORE. SHE FUCKS TOURISTS—THAT'S WHAT SHE DOES—WHAT FUCKING WORLD ARE YOU LIVING IN!?

BILL: Okay, okay: listen—

LEE: I mean, come on, how sheltered can *one person* be?

BILL: Both of you: stop it.

JUSTINE: You're disgusting.

LEE: Yeah?

JUSTINE: Yeah.

LEE: So? So what?

JUSTINE: You're *sick*.

LEE: SO'S EVERYONE! THAT'S WHY THERE ARE *A BILLION TEENAGE PROSTI-TUTES ON EARTH*!

BILL: Honey—

JUSTINE: *(to LEE)* Fuck you.

BILL: Justine, calm down, you're losing your temper.

JUSTINE: OF COURSE I'M LOSING MY TEMPER, and now you're going to take his side! YOU LOVE HIM. YOU LOVE HIM: you spend all your time with him. Well I'm your daughter, so please TAKE MY SIDE FOR ONCE BECAUSE YOU'RE GOING TO DO WHAT YOU ALWAYS DO, WHICH IS SIT THERE QUIETLY AND WATCH US FIGHT AND THEN YOU'RE GOING TO TAKE HIS SIDE.

BILL: Justine, it isn't about sides—

JUSTINE: Please take the side of your daughter over *a child molester*!

LEE: What the fuck: can I go?

BILL: *(to JUSTINE)* Hey. Hey.

JUSTINE: I am FINE! I am FINE, I am just . . .

BILL: Hey.

JUSTINE: I want to find that girl and . . .

BILL: It's all right.

JUSTINE: *(low)* I am . . . !

BILL: Sh sh.

JUSTINE: I . . .

BILL: Shhhh.

Beat.

JUSTINE: And fuck, Shannon?! How could you!

SHANNON freezes.

How could you listen to him say all that and not be disgusted and be . . . telling my dad everything you said to me last night . . . ! You should have some . . . ! Compassion for her? A little girl?

Beat.

You've been through it.

A standoff.

During which LEE *looks up at* SHANNON, *and then glances between the two women.*

LEE: You have?

SHANNON: I . . . ? No, I haven't?

JUSTINE: *(to* SHANNON, *but directed to* LEE *and* BILL*)* Shannon had a step-dad who molested her when she was fourteen years old, so if anyone should give a fuck about what happened to this girl, it's Shannon.

Beat.

LEE *and* BILL *are both staring at* SHANNON *now.*

Beat.

LEE: *(low, to* SHANNON*)* I didn't . . . I didn't . . . know that?

SHANNON: *(to* JUSTINE*)* That—that's . . .

Beat.

That—

JUSTINE: This is a girl, who was young, who Lee hurt in some way / that . . .

SHANNON: *(to* JUSTINE*)* You can't tell them that.

JUSTINE: Shannon, come on. You get shit-faced and you let Lee fuck you—then you come to my hotel room and you've got vomit on you and you're saying he's hurt a little girl, then you don't want / to tell my father that that's what he said: you want to keep it all quiet—

SHANNON: You . . . can't tell them that. I mean that's . . . That's not a joke, you can't . . .

Beat.

I told you that when—when I was not . . . good—

JUSTINE: *(to SHANNON)* YOU'RE COVERING UP A CHILD BEING MOLESTED!

SHANNON: I . . . I . . . don't . . . like to—like it wasn't . . . I don't . . . like my mom still . . . doesn't know—

JUSTINE: Tell my dad what Lee said.

SHANNON: I don't know what you're angry at me for. I haven't done anything except for have my personal information told to the CEO and COO of my company—

JUSTINE: I'm angry because: tell my dad what Lee said—

BILL: Justine, come on, stop—

JUSTINE: She's ashamed of what happened with her stepdad, which: fine, makes no sense, but fine. It's also why she likes Lee: 'cause he's a child molester and she's reliving her shitty childhood with him.

LEE: Jesus fuck.

SHANNON: I . . .

BILL: *(to SHANNON)* Shannon, I'm sorry, it—it's gone too far.

LEE: *(to JUSTINE)* You're treating your employee like shit.

JUSTINE: *(to LEE)* Oh fuck you—'cause fucking Shannon the night after you fucked a child is treating her well?

LEE: She's upset. Look at her.

JUSTINE: She was upset last night, Lee.

SHANNON: *(to BILL, looking at the floor)* Would uh . . . if . . . ? I'd like to . . . ?

SHANNON points at the door.

BILL nods.

Before SHANNON runs out:

JUSTINE: Fine, I'm sorry! I'm sorry—I, look: I shouldn't have . . . said that.

Beat.

I'm sorry, I'm . . . being a bad . . . I'm sorry.

SHANNON: I . . . look, I don't want to . . . talk about this anymore.

JUSTINE: Yeah, okay, yeah.

SHANNON turns to BILL.

SHANNON: I'd like to go.

BILL: Of course.

SHANNON runs out.

JUSTINE: *(to BILL)* Dad, you have to fire him.

BILL: Justine—

JUSTINE: You have to fire him, you have to tell the board, and you have to fire him.

BILL: Justine, I have something / to—

JUSTINE: WHAT DO YOU EVEN LIKE ABOUT HIM? HE'S YOUR FIFTH FUCKING COUSIN? WHAT DO YOU LIKE ABOUT HIM? Because I can't—I can't—

BILL: Listen: listen to me, look me in the eyes—okay, listen—

JUSTINE: Do you think this is the only time, like WHAT THE FUCK WAS HE DOING THE WHOLE TIME HE WAS IN SHENZHEN?

LEE: WORKING!!!!!

BILL: No. Listen—Justine—!

JUSTINE: He's been up to my lake. He sat in my hot tub.

BILL: It's difficult, Justine: I'm sure you know from your charity work that in these countries where there aren't the same kind of opportunities that we're used to, sometimes girls do end up in prostitution—

JUSTINE: He's been near Chloe!

LEE: She's four years old.

JUSTINE: *(to LEE)* THAT'S MY POINT.

LEE: WOW! WOW! OKAY, WOW! YOU KNOW WHAT? WHAT IS THIS ABOUT? BECAUSE I CAN TAKE SOME GOOD GUESSES?

JUSTINE: It's about you fucking children.

LEE: He loves you more than he loves me, okay? *He loves you more.* Whatever your bullshit insecurity sad story is around your dad, I am sick of you taking it out on me.

JUSTINE: Yeah. Yeah. At least when I get insecure I don't go and *have sex with a child.*

LEE: I just said to you that he loves you more than me! What more do you want? Is this some Asian thing, / like you'll never feel loved because you're Asian? Is that what this is? Come on. Let's figure out *what the fuck is wrong with you.*

   Simultaneous:

BILL: Both of you . . . ! I am . . . I . . .

JUSTINE: Oh fuck you. You're so fucked up about my dad and his approval and getting in with my dad and where's your dad and have you seen your dad—

LEE: YOU WIN!

JUSTINE: You know what? You're a loser. / Let's figure out what the fuck is wrong with you. Fucking listening to hip hop in your Maserati . . .

LEE: . . . Yeah, exactly, you just *hate me—yeah, you hate me, drop this self-righteous I-give-a-shit about people . . .*

JUSTINE: Like maybe ask yourself WHY YOU FUCKED A CHILD. WHY DID YOU DO IT, LEE—WHY—WHAT PART OF YOUR FUCKED-UP PSYCHE— and yeah I hate you because you're a total piece of shit and fuck you I might have some reason for giving a shit about these people, like who do you think my birth parents were / and why do you think they gave me up?

LEE: Oh oh, I get it, you're all "these people are JUST LIKE ME!!!!!" BUT GUESS WHAT!? YOU ARE A FUCKING CFO OF A MASSIVE CAR CORPORATION. YOU THREW A SIXTY-THOUSAND DOLLAR PARTY FOR YOUR FOUR-YEAR-OLD. YOU MADE A DOG JUMP OUT OF A CAKE. YOU HAVE NO FUCKING IDEA WHAT THEIR LIVES ARE. *I* HAVE A BETTER IDEA OF THEIR LIVES THAN YOU. I'M THE ONE WHO WAS *WITH HER . . . I KNOW WHAT SHE SMELLS LIKE AND LOOKS LIKE WHEN SHE'S . . .*

Silence.

JUSTINE: *(to BILL, low)* Fire him.

BILL: Yeah.

Beat.

I can't.

Beat.

Justine, no, look at me, not at him, and listen: I'd like to fire Lee, but I can't and here's why.

JUSTINE: WHY NOT.

BILL: Because—

JUSTINE: WHAT! Go to the board and tell them *all this. I'll tell them*—

BILL: Because . . . Justine, I'm sorry to have to tell you in these . . . This isn't . . .

Beat.

JUSTINE: What?

Beat.

What? What?

BILL: I had a biopsy and . . .

Beat.

I'm going to have to step down for a . . . short while, to undergo treatment.

Beat.

JUSTINE: Dad.

Beat.

BILL: Yeah.

Beat.

JUSTINE: What.

Beat.

I mean . . . really?

LEE: Nah, he's fucking with you about *having cancer.*

Beat.

JUSTINE: What . . . kind?

BILL: It's in my lungs.

Beat.

JUSTINE: What's the prognosis?

BILL shrugs.

Beat.

Is it a bad one?

BILL: You'll . . . look it up.

JUSTINE: Why? It's a bad one?

Beat.

BILL: Yeah.

Beat.

JUSTINE: You . . . What?

Beat.

What's the . . . ? What's the treatment plan?

BILL: I have . . . uh . . . a good medical team, and this'll have to be made public, and I need Lee in place, as part of the transition, so.

Beat.

JUSTINE: Dad.

BILL: Yeah.

JUSTINE: How—how long have you known?

BILL: Five days.

Beat.

I've been . . . having a hard time . . . sleeping.

JUSTINE: Oh my god, Dad. Oh my god.

Beat.

I'm *sorry.*

BILL: *Yeah.*

JUSTINE: Should . . . should you be here?

BILL: I . . . listen, I'm trying to get this sorted out, so I can . . . go.

Beat.

The board likes this deal, with Systemas. They'll appoint Lee to the position, pending this deal.

Beat.

The other choice is that the company goes out of direct family control, we bring in an interim CEO, and there is a possibility that I . . . don't come back and . . .

Beat.

. . . And that CEO stays. The final decision'll be up to the board if I'm gone and I know—I know what your objections are to Lee, and they're real, I heard you yesterday about our . . . company culture, and Lee's . . . lack of responsiveness there, and today: this. Which—look, it isn't good. I was . . . hoping you and Lee would find . . . common—I wanted you to come tour Systemas to get your insights and so that you would be part of the . . . And, yeah, there are substantial downsides with Lee, but I think the alternative is worse. I've spent a lot of years—most of the years of my life—remember when you gave me that photo album of your childhood, Justine, and there were no photos of me in it: I was at your adoption and then I was at your graduation and the rest was you and your mother. I've probably made bad decisions, but I do give a shit about what happens to this company. I do give a shit about handing it down to Chloe in good shape. That's what I'm thinking about. Listen, honey, don't cry. We're going to sit down and you can ask me all the questions . . . you have. Look, if we'd had more . . . time, we would have . . . I'd be . . . getting you the general management experience that you would have needed, and . . . this would be . . . a different conversation . . . one with you more involved. And you'll still hold your seat on the board, and you can . . . vote against Lee . . . and look, I'm . . . I don't like how sure I am that the board would not approve you. They would, I think, point to your lack of managerial experience and . . . maybe . . . something . . . that they wouldn't be able to wholly articulate that . . . would . . . factor in, and that would be . . . the worst . . . part of them that would look at you and think . . . "no."

Beat.

Let's get this deal finalized with Systemas: I know Lee feels badly about the incident. He admitted to me that there was a question about the girl's age. Justine, Justine, look at me, not at Lee, this is between you and me now. The girl did come to the door and present herself as a prostitute . . . *(off JUSTINE's reaction)* Wait, wait: no, here's what's going to happen. Lee's going to make a donation to your charity work. You can make sure the funds reach other young girls, at your clinics.

Silence.

Silence.

JUSTINE: *(to BILL)* It would have to be a lot. It would have to be *a lot.*

BILL: . . . *(shrugs, nods)* Yeah.

JUSTINE: A lot.

BILL: How much?

JUSTINE: *(looking at LEE but speaking to BILL)* Ten mill.

LEE walks away.

I'll list him as one of my major donors. And he fires Gary himself.

Beat.

Is he sorry or not?

BILL: *(to LEE)* He's sorry. He's going to pay the ten mill. He'll fire Gary.

Beat.

He made a mistake.

End scene.

Scene Five.

The lounge. Night. BILL sits, scrolling on his phone. LEE comes in, stands, waits. BILL beckons him over.

LEE: Can I get you . . . ? Something? Can I do something?

BILL: Cure cancer.

LEE: Yeah!

BILL: I'll have a drink.

LEE: Yeah.

LEE pours them both a drink from the bar.

How's Justine?

BILL shrugs.

How did the talk go?

BILL shrugs.

BILL: She wants me to be around, see Chloe grow up. I said: "I want that too."

LEE: Yeah.

Beat.

We own Systemas.

BILL nods. They clink glasses.

BILL: Connor's been working on the succession plan—it'll name you the interim CEO, I'll go to the board with it as soon as we're home— I'm hoping approval will be . . . quick. I'll stay on as Chairman of the Board. I'm going to suggest that you choose a COO from your own people, so you have someone you work well with.

LEE: Thank you.

Beat.

And thanks for the job.

They smile.

I wish it wasn't in these circumstances.

BILL: Me too.

LEE: Yeah!

Beat.

BILL: I want you to . . . look after Justine, and Chloe.

Beat.

LEE: Yeah.

Beat.

Yeah. And uh Shannon is going to uh—I—uh—I shouldn't have uh . . . Well listen at this point, but uh Shannon . . . I talked it over with her, and she's going to tender her resignation, because of the conflict of interest, because she and I are . . . Yeah. Wanted to tell you that.

Pause.

BILL: Lee.

LEE: Yah!

BILL: The girl?

Beat.

You said to Justine that you paid her? The girl? You said you paid her?

LEE: Yeah?

BILL: Systemas paid her.

Beat.

Systemas wanted us to buy Systemas: it was a sweetener, they paid her.

LEE: Oh. Yeah. They did. I tipped her.

BILL: Yeah? Why?

LEE shrugs.

There is a standoff between BILL and LEE.

LEE: She earned it.

BILL: How?

LEE shrugs.

Beat.

LEE shrugs.

Pause.

LEE: Yeah? You're asking?

BILL: I'm—yeah.

LEE: Why?

Beat.

Is it a liability thing? Will it change . . . ?

BILL: No . . .

LEE: . . . The succession plan? No?

BILL: In normal circumstances, maybe, but: no.

Beat.

LEE: Look, I . . . Okay. Okay.

Pause.

Okay.

BILL: Was she hurt?

LEE: Uh. Uh. *Maybe.* There was blood, but I think uh it was her first time, and not because I hurt her, although I can't one hundred percent rule that out, there was a, you know, language barrier. I was asking her if she was okay, because she cried, uh, after, and, uh, during, but I think that was emotional rather than physical. Then she walked out.

Beat.

That's it.

Beat.

(to himself, almost) I . . . yeah, she seemed . . . I was looking at her . . . during it, and I was like, "Why does this remind me of middle school?" And . . . I was like, "I wonder if she's too young, what am I doing?" But I didn't . . . stop . . . ? I don't know why I didn't . . . uh . . . stop?

Beat.

I don't have a good answer.

Beat.

Sorry.

Beat.

Can I go? Can I uh—I'm going to go?

BILL: Yeah.

LEE stands up and goes toward the exit.

BILL sits there thinking.

LEE turns back.

LEE: Oh, right, Bill, I wanted to say thank you for . . . the job, and the trust in me, and for mediating between Justine and me, so I bought you that painting.

LEE points at the wall.

You seemed to like it, so . . .

Beat.

It's yours.

Beat.

LEE goes out.

BILL stands up slowly.

He goes over to the art on the wall.

He gazes at it.

End scene.

End play.

Acknowledgements.

The author would like to acknowledge the support of Prairie Theatre Exchange, and in particular the significant contribution Thomas Morgan Jones made to the development of the play.

Early scenes of *Post-Democracy* were performed at Volcano Theatre's Wrecking Ball, the Rhubarb Festival at Buddies in Bad Times Theatre, and at Playwrights Theatre Centre Vancouver. The play was commissioned by Robert Metcalfe at Prairie Theatre Exchange, and was developed at the Banff Playwrights Lab. A workshop at Canadian Stage's RAW! Festival was supported through grants from the Toronto Arts Council and the Ontario Arts Council.

Hannah Moscovitch is an acclaimed Canadian playwright, TV writer, and librettist whose work has been widely produced in Canada and around the world. Recent stage work includes *Sexual Misconduct of the Middle Classes* and *Old Stock: A Refugee Love Story* (co-created with Christian Barry and Ben Caplan). Hannah has been the recipient of numerous awards, including the Governor General's Literary Award for Drama, the Trillium Book Award, the Nova Scotia Masterworks Arts Award, the Scotsman Fringe First and the Herald Angel Awards at the Edinburgh Festival Fringe, and the prestigious Windham-Campbell Prize administered by Yale University. She has been nominated for the international Susan Smith Blackburn Prize, the Drama Desk Award, and Canada's Siminovitch Prize in Theatre. She is a playwright-in-residence at Tarragon Theatre in Toronto. She spends her time between Halifax and Los Angeles.